OUTDOOR WONDERLAND

The Kids' Guide to Being Outside

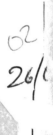

First published in the UK in 2014 by

Ivy Press

210 High Street

Lewes

East Sussex BN7 2NS

United Kingdom

www.ivypress.co.uk

ISBN: 978-1-78240-082-0

This book was conceived, designed & produced by

Ivy Press

CREATIVE DIRECTOR	Peter Bridgewater
MANAGING EDITOR	Hazel Songhurst
COMMISSIONING EDITOR	Georgia Amson-Bradshaw
PROJECT EDITOR	Dereen Taylor
ART DIRECTOR	Kim Hankinson
DESIGNERS	Clare Barber and Kevin Knight
ILLUSTRATOR	Alice Lickens

Text by Josie Jeffery and Dereen Taylor

Printed in China

Colour origination by Ivy Press Reprographics

10 9 8 7 6 5 4 3 2 1

Competent adult supervision is required for many of the activities
in this book. All safety and supervision advice given should be fully
adhered to. Every effort has been made to ensure that all information
in this book is accurate. Neither the publisher nor the author can be
held responsible for any injury, loss or other damages which may
result from the use of information in this book.

OUTDOOR WONDERLAND

The Kids' Guide to Being Outside

Josie Jeffery

Illustrated by
Alice Lickens

Ivy KidS

Contents

WINDY DAYS

RAINY DAYS

SUNNY DAYS

BY THE WATER

IN THE STREET

About This Book

Are you always being told to go outdoors and play, but don't know what to do once you get there? Well, help is here! This book is packed with exciting activities and adventures, giving you all the ideas you need to make the most of the amazing outdoor wonderland on your doorstep.

The book is divided into sections with fun activity ideas for all weathers, so rain won't have to stop play any more! There are also sections with activities for wherever you are — whether it's the park, the garden, the woods, by water, in the street, and even after darkness falls.

So whatever the weather, and whether you're in a sleepy village, the urban jungle, by the shore, or deep in the countryside, this book has all you need to keep your friends, family and YOU busy all through the day, and even after dark!

With so many awesome activities, you'll never be bored again - just grab this book and explore the outdoor wonderland!

What shall we do today?

You could head into the woods and build a den, or design a bug hotel for your outdoor space. Why not organize a Park Olympics day, an urban animal safari, or a street party? If you're feeling artistic, you could create cloud art, rain paintings or mossy woodland sculptures. Or if you're in the mood for learning a new skill, try skimming the perfect pebble, play the grass trumpet, or learn how to become a wildlife photographer. And if you're still looking for something to do after sunset, you could enjoy a star-spotting session or watch an enchanting performance at the moth theatre.

Helper Bug

When Helper Bug appears, you need an adult to give you assistance. This will ensure top results!

Danger Bug

When Danger Bug appears, be extra careful! An adult MUST supervise the activity to keep you safe.

It's time to get yourself outside & have some FUN!

Grow It, Eat It!

If you've ever picked your own strawberries you'll know how much better they taste than strawberries bought in the shops. So just imagine how stupendously scrumptious strawberries that you've actually grown yourself will be.

Berry backpack

You can grow your strawberries in special grow-bags or in pots… or you could try something a bit different, and plant them in an old backpack instead!

When the strawberries are red and juicy, they are ready to pick and eat! YUM, YUM!

YOU WILL NEED

- Backpack with pockets
- Screwdriver
- Pebbles or small stones
- Compost
- Perlite
- Trowel
- Strawberry plants (enough to fill all the pockets)
- Garden netting
- Watering can
- Plant food
- An adult helper

Birds beware!

To make sure that birds don't eat all your strawberries before you do, you can make a brilliant bird scarer using string, old CDs and kitchen foil. Thread a CD onto the string, and then cover the string either side of it with a twist of foil about 5cm long. Carry on alternating the CDs and the foil until the string is full. Hang your bird scarer above your strawberry plants by tying it between two garden canes. Ta dah!

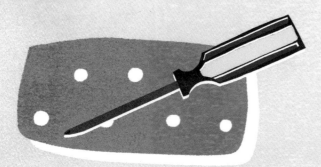

1 Ask an adult to make small holes in the base of the backpack and at the bottom of the pockets using a screwdriver. Place the backpack in a sunny spot, out of the wind.

2 Put a layer of pebbles or stones in the base and in the pockets for drainage. Then top up with compost mixed with a handful of perlite. The perlite helps the compost to stay moist.

3 Dig holes in the compost with your trowel and drop the plants in, then cover the roots with compost. Carefully pat down the compost around the plants, and water.

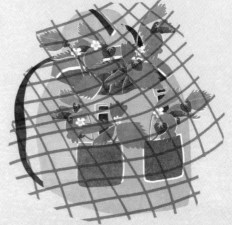

4 Cover loosely with netting to stop birds munching on the berries. Water daily, and when white flowers appear, feed once a week. These flowers will eventually turn into fruits.

Bee Friendly!

Bees are super important when it comes to helping things grow – in fact we'd be in big trouble without them. You can get to know your busy little visitors better, and help them out, by making your garden a bee-friendly haven.

Busy bee survey

Here's how to find out how many bees buzz through your garden each day. You need paper and coloured pens, and a spot where some bee-friendly flowering plants grow.

Down the side of your paper, mark the information you want to survey. You could count the different types of bees that visit, and which plants they like the most. Along the top, mark the times when you will be surveying. Stay for ten minutes each time, and count how many bees come buzzing by…

Tip Try not to be too noisy or move too suddenly, or you will disturb the bees!

NUMBER OF VISITS

Types of bee	8am	12pm
Honeybee		
Bumblebee		
Carpenter bee		

Go green

If you really want to get your garden buzzing, try planting scented open-flowered plants such as alliums, daisies, lavender, oriental poppies and snapdragons.

BUZZ

BUZZ

Bees at work

Bees do a really important job in your garden. As they buzz around your plants, they pass pollen from one flower to another. This is called 'pollination', and it is how many flowering plants make seeds to grow into new plants. About one third of everything we eat is pollinated by bees!

4PM	7PM	Plants visited

LAVENDER

SNAPDRAGON

Bee fact

There are about 20,000 different species of bees in the world!

Ready, Set, GROW!

Are you a green-fingered gardening wizard? Growing plants may seem a bit like magic, especially when bulbs sprout up months after you planted them, but really it's super easy!

YOU WILL NEED

- A sunny, grassy area to plant your spiral
- 2 x 7-metre long marker ropes
- Lots of bulbs (around 50 bulbs per square metre)
- A shovel
- An adult helper

Amazing bulb spiral

Lots of different types of flowers grow from bulbs, including hyacinths, daffodils, tulips and bluebells. Bulbs 'sleep' underground until the time is right for them to grow and to flower. You can't see them until they sprout, so it's fun to plant 'invisible' patterns during autumn, that will magically appear in the spring.

One great project you can do over a few days is to plant a flower spiral that you can walk around. The steps show you how to make a spiral around 2 metres wide.

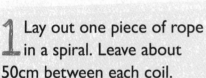

1 Lay out one piece of rope in a spiral. Leave about 50cm between each coil.

2 Lay out the second rope next to the first, so they are about 25cm apart.

3 Dig a trench between the ropes. It should be 20cm wide and twice the depth of your bulbs. Place the turf you remove to the side.

4 Lay your bulbs in the trench a few inches apart. Make sure the roots are facing downward.

5 Fill in the trench and replace the turf, then lightly press down with your feet.

6 When you have planted the bulbs all the way along your spiral, water it well. Then, just wait for the flowers to appear in spring!

Tip In a big garden, you can increase the scale of your spiral by doubling the quantities of rope and bulbs.

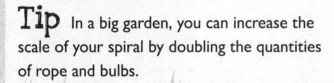

Flower Power

Flowers only last a few days once you've picked them, but there is a simple way to make them last much longer – flower pressing. It will keep your love of nature blooming!

Press to impress!

The simplest way to press flowers is between the pages of a heavy book. Remember to protect the book's pages from staining by placing the flower between two sheets of tissue paper first.

Follow the top tips shown on the petals below, and you'll be well on your way to pressing success.

Choose flowers with simple shapes

Try just pressing petals

Make sure flowers are dry

Leave for two weeks

Lay leaves out flat

Always ask before you pick

Pick different shaped flowers

Press flowers soon after picking

Sparkling sun catcher

Once your pressed flowers are ready, you can make a sparkling sun catcher to show them off.

YOU WILL NEED

- A selection of pressed flowers
- 2 x small, clear acrylic blocks (10cm x 10cm)
- Toothpick
- Glue (clear drying is best)
- Coloured electrical tape (2.5cm thick)
- Scissors
- 10cm of picture wire
- Ribbon
- An adult helper

1 Place your pressed flowers onto the flat side of one of the acrylic blocks, picking one corner as the 'top' of your picture.

2 Using the toothpick, carefully stick the flowers in place with tiny dots of glue. Leave the glue to dry.

3 Cut four strips of tape slightly longer than the sides of the blocks. Put the second block on top of the flowers and wrap tape around the bottom two sides to hold the blocks together. Make sure the tape is straight.

4 Bend the picture wire to make a loop at the top, leaving two long ends at the bottom pointing out.

5 Position the loop at the top corner and place the wire ends along the sides. Neatly tape over these ends as you wrap tape around the top two sides of the layered blocks.

6 Trim the tape at the corners and tie a ribbon onto the loop. Then hang your sun catcher in the window and watch it sparkle!

At The Bug Hotel

Get insects and other animals checking in to their own luxury hotel by building a cosy habitat for them to shelter in over the winter. This recycled shelter will cost nothing to make… but it will be worth a heap to your guests!

The big build

✱ Start off by building the frame. Place crates or pallets on top of each other, or use old planks of wood layered up on bricks. Turn the gaps into guest rooms by putting in paper tubes, pebbles, potted plants, upside-down flower pots, logs, bricks and roof tiles.

✱ Decorate each 'room' with dry leaves, straw, twigs, moss, feathers, fir cones and bark – anything that will keep your guests sheltered and warm.

Frogs and toads will hop under bricks and tiles.

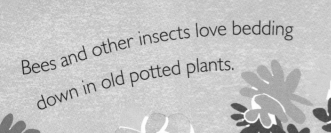
Bees and other insects love bedding down in old potted plants.

Be an insect expert

Entomologists are insect experts. You can be an entomologist too, by keeping a close eye on one type of insect that visits your hotel. Do they check in alone, or with other guests? Do they build a nest – or bed down in the comfy surroundings? By the end of their stay, you will know much more about your chosen insect and their habits.

Tip This is a great group activity, so ask friends and family to choose a 'room' to decorate!

Dawn and Dusk

What's the difference between day and night? Is it just levels of light? Check out the wildlife in your garden at each end of the day, and you'll find there's much more to it than that…

What is dawn?

Dawn is the first appearance of light before sunrise, early in the morning.

Birdsong

You may have heard of bird-watching, but have you heard of bird-listening? It's when you close your eyes and really listen to the sounds that birds make.

At dawn, birds sing more loudly than they do at other times of the day, and the air is often cooler and stiller, making the sounds easier to hear. This is called the 'dawn chorus', and it is best heard during spring. Different birds have different calls and songs – some even sound like they are speaking! Listen carefully to what the birds are saying in your garden. It may surprise you!

GET RECORDING

You could try recording the sounds made by wildlife in your garden at dawn and at dusk and compare your findings.

- When is it noisiest?

- What is the noisiest animal at dawn, and at dusk?

- What kind of wildlife is most active at dawn – birds or other types of animals?

What is dusk?

Dusk is the period at the end of the day between light and darkness.

Getting dark

In many places, it takes around 30 minutes to get dark after the sun has set, but this varies depending on where you are. You can find out how long it takes where you live by timing from the moment the sun sets, until total darkness. Once darkness has fallen, find a quiet spot and see what nocturnal visitors to your garden you can see – or hear.

Bat fact

Bats emerge from their daytime roosts at dusk. They have poor eyesight and use echolocation – this means they send out high-pitched beeps and listen for changes in the echoes that bounce back at them. This allows them to work out which direction to go in and where to find their food.

GET EXPERIMENTING

Ask friends and family around the country, or even the world, to join in an experiment to see if it takes the same length of time to get dark in different places. There's a useful website on page 76 that tells you what time the sun will set in your neighbourhood.

The Sun Goes Down

Just because it's getting dark doesn't mean it's time to head indoors. You can still make the most of the amazing outdoors as darkness falls!

Sunset silhouette painting

There's only one way to describe a spectacular, fiery sky at sunset – wow! Sunset happens daily as the sun disappears below the horizon, but sometimes, when the conditions are right, it creates stunning, dramatic colours in the sky. Here's one way of capturing that perfect moment of colour and natural beauty.

YOU WILL NEED

- A beautiful sunset to inspire you
- White paper
- Paints, pastels or coloured chalks
- Paintbrush
- Easel or board

1 Pick a building or tree that stands out against the sky. As the light dims, the object will become darker, until it is a silhouette. It is this contrast between the black outline and the colourful sky that will make your picture dramatic.

2 Place your piece of paper on an easel or board, and paint your sunset background using red, pink and orange colours. Leave it to dry.

3 Using black paint, carefully paint the outline of the silhouette over the colourful background, trying to keep it really sharp, then fill it in.

Torch tag

Fancy a game of 'tag!' with a fun night-time twist? All you need is a group of at least three friends with torches and a safe, dark space to play in. The more friends playing and the more places there are to hide, the better the game will be. It's about stealth and tactics rather than simply outrunning the person who is 'it'.

Tip Make sure you flash your torch on and off super fast, so that you don't get spotted!

1 Everyone has one minute to run off in different directions with their torches (which are switched off).

2 Taking care not to be seen, each player goes on a hunt for their friends.

3 If someone manages to sneak up and shine their torch on another player then that player is out!

4 Step 3 repeats until only one stealthy tagger is left – and they are the winner of the game!

Twinkle, Twinkle...

Look up on a clear, cloud-free night… the sky is alive with twinkling stars! Each one is trillions of miles away. The light coming from them has taken many years to reach us.

Join the star dots

If you know what you are looking for, you can see star groups, called constellations. Ask an adult to help you find star maps and star-gazing advice on the internet.

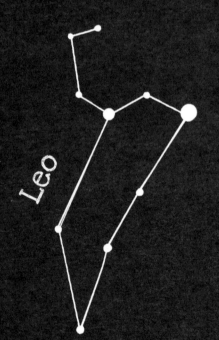

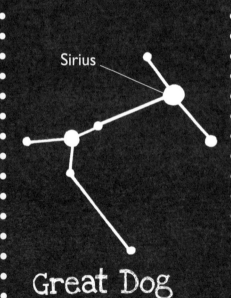

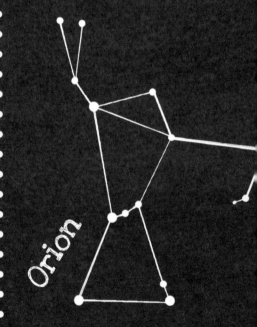

The constellation of Leo represents a lion. The part that looks like a back-to-front question mark is the lion's head. Leo can be seen most clearly during the months of March, April and May.

The Great Dog constellation is easy to recognise as it contains the brightest star in the entire night sky – Sirius. The Great Dog is most clearly visible during January, February and March.

Orion is one of the easiest constellations to spot. It has an hourglass shape, with a 3-star band, Orion's Belt, in the middle. It is most clearly visible during December, January and February.

Be a star expert

An astronomer is a scientist who studies moons, planets and stars – and you can be one tonight! Check out the moon and, using the chart here, work out where it is in its monthly cycle. Is it nearer to the full moon (complete moon visible), or the new moon (no moon visible)? See if you can track the moon for a month, and each night draw what you see or take a photograph to record your very own moon cycle!

Star struck
There is one star you can always see during the day – the sun! It is the star at the centre of our solar system.

Meteor showers

If you watch the sky from a dark location, you may see dazzling streaks of light from meteors, or 'shooting stars'. These are pieces of space debris burning up when they get close to the earth. Several times a year, comets pass close to the earth, leaving a stream of debris which makes a stunning meteor shower.

The Secret Garden

Shh… it's bedtime… but not for everyone! Outside is a whole new place at night, with nocturnal creatures getting out of their beds just as you are getting ready for yours.

A moth theatre

Moths have beautiful wings like butterflies, but most only come out at night. You've probably seen them fluttering around streetlamps – they are attracted to bright lights. You can use this behaviour to get them to put on a fabulous show just for you!

YOU WILL NEED

- A large white sheet and permission to paint on it
- Coloured paints
- Clothes line and pegs to hang up your sheet
- Heavy stones to weigh down the bottom of the sheet
- A bright white light (either a tall lamp or a bright torch)
- A comfortable chair – and some popcorn

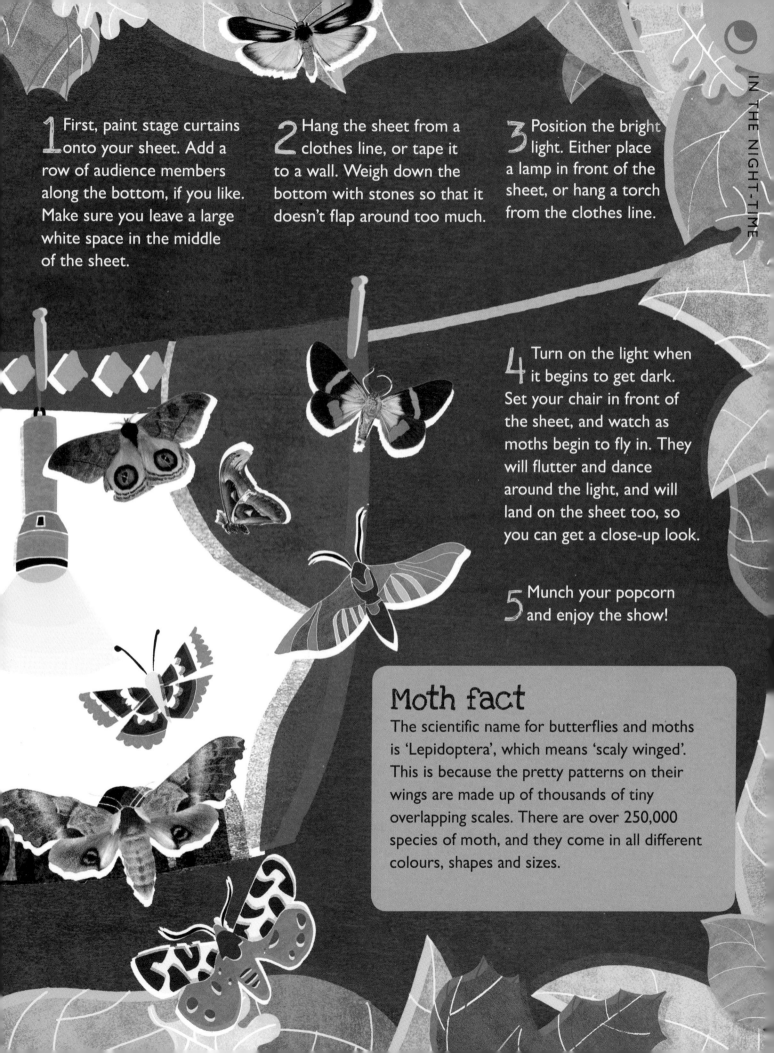

1 First, paint stage curtains onto your sheet. Add a row of audience members along the bottom, if you like. Make sure you leave a large white space in the middle of the sheet.

2 Hang the sheet from a clothes line, or tape it to a wall. Weigh down the bottom with stones so that it doesn't flap around too much.

3 Position the bright light. Either place a lamp in front of the sheet, or hang a torch from the clothes line.

4 Turn on the light when it begins to get dark. Set your chair in front of the sheet, and watch as moths begin to fly in. They will flutter and dance around the light, and will land on the sheet too, so you can get a close-up look.

5 Munch your popcorn and enjoy the show!

Moth fact

The scientific name for butterflies and moths is 'Lepidoptera', which means 'scaly winged'. This is because the pretty patterns on their wings are made up of thousands of tiny overlapping scales. There are over 250,000 species of moth, and they come in all different colours, shapes and sizes.

Park Life

It's really easy to spend a terrific day at the park. With the great ideas in this section, you won't even think about heading for the swings and slides!

Climb a tree

Make sure an adult is standing by! Find a tree with strong, large branches that can support your weight. To stay safe, keep three of your limbs on the tree at all times. Look for holes to hook into with your hands and feet, and smaller branches that you can use as footholds. Take it slowly and enjoy the view.

Grass trumpets

Pick a thin, flat blade of grass, from a nice clean spot. Press your thumbs together side-to-side, with the grass sandwiched between them. Place your lips against your thumbs and slowly blow through the gap – you'll hear a surprisingly loud sound!

Park survival basics

Before you head off to the park, make sure you're kitted out with plenty of picnic rations, and don't forget the all-important picnic blanket – perfect for canopy making, as well as for sitting on!

At the park, scout out the best terrain for your base camp. On a hot day, a shady spot under a tree is best. You can drape your blanket on low branches to make your canopy.

Water will stay cooler for longer 'buried' in the soil. Just make sure the bottle is well sealed!

Safety

Look after others and always climb down with your body facing the tree.

Go green

Don't forget to put litter in the bin after your picnic.

On Your Marks

The great thing about the park is that there's so much space for everyone to race about — it's the perfect place to stage your very own Park Olympics. The more people that are competing, the better! You could try these events…

Walking wardrobe

YOU WILL NEED

- Two sets of clothing and accessories (things you have at the park — two pairs of sunglasses, two sweatshirts, etc)
- Two teams

✳ Lay out the sets of clothes in two parallel lines, with around one metre between each item. The first players from each team race to put on and then take off each item as quickly as they can. They then run back and tag the next player to go.

My shoe flew!

YOU WILL NEED

- A clear, open space
- A shoe to throw
- A group of throwers, each with a pebble or lolly stick to use as a marker

✳ Take it in turns to see who can throw the shoe the furthest.

✳ Each player should mark their landing spot with a marker.

✳ Use clothing to form circles, then land a shoe inside a circle to win extra kudos!

Capture the flag

* The playing area is divided into three – one territory belonging to each team, and a neutral space (belonging to neither) in the middle. Each territory has a small 'jail' section.

* Each team secretly hides their flag in their territory. Players must find and grab the opposing team's flag without getting caught on enemy territory.

* If a player finds an enemy team member on their team's territory, they may take them to jail. A player can only be freed from jail by a member of their own team touching them.

* The winning team is the one who captures the other team's flag and brings it back to their own territory.

Red rover

* The teams form two parallel lines opposite each other. Each team joins hands to create a chain.

* The captain of Team A chooses a player from Team B and invites them to play by calling, 'Red Rover, Red Rover, let (choose a player) come over!'

* The chosen player then runs at the opposing team and tries to break through their chain.

* If the player fails, they join that chain, and the Team A captain chooses another player to take a turn.

* If the player succeeds, they go back to Team B, and choose a player from Team A to take a turn breaking their chain.

* The game ends when one team has all but one of the players in their chain.

Wild Photography

The best way to really see the park and all the creatures that live in it is to get behind a camera. It is guaranteed to make you view your surroundings in a new way. So get ready to zoom in on nature!

Picture this!

There's so much to see in the park – trees, flowers, birds, and other animals. With the tips below and a bit of practice, you'll be photographing them all like a pro in no time!

Up close
Use the zoom to get in close and capture every amazing detail.

Keep shooting
Take lots of shots to make sure you get that one perfect image.

Get an angle on it
Take pictures from unusual angles and viewpoints.

Focus
Place your camera on a steady surface to keep your images sharp.

PHOTO FUN

When you get home, don't forget to download or print your photos. You could create a collage on screen, or keep them in an album. Print out an extra set and use your photos to play some cool games, like the ones explained on the next page.

Zoom!

If you've taken some mega-zoomed-in shots, you can test your friends' knowledge of nature by seeing if they can recognize what you photographed!

Snap!

Cut your pictures in half, shuffle them and split them into two packs. Use them to play a wild game of 'Snap!'

Pairs

Halved pictures are also perfect for a game of pairs. Mix them up and spread them out, face-down. Take it in turns to try to flip over two matching halves.

Be a wildlife photographer

A wildlife photographer travels the world taking pictures of wild animals in their natural habitats. And you can be one too! Patience is essential… and keeping quiet and still. You need to sneak up on the animal you want to photograph, or sit very still and wait for it to come to you. If the animal sees you or hears you, it will run away and you will lose your shot!

Nature Spotter

The woods are full of animals and plant life, and even wild food! So keep your eyes peeled and see what you can spot…

BIRDS

Bird tracks normally show three toes pointing forward, and one back.

Get tracking!

Have you ever been at the beach and seen footprints in the sand? Maybe you followed them to find out where they went – this is called 'tracking'.

You can't always see animals in the wild, but you can find out a lot from what they leave behind. By looking at their footprints, a sharp-eyed tracker can tell what sort of animal passed by, and where they were going. The best place to look for animal tracks is on soft ground, such as mud, snow or sand.

FOX

If you see a paw print with little dots at the front, it is an animal that can't pull in its claws, like a dog or a fox.

DEER

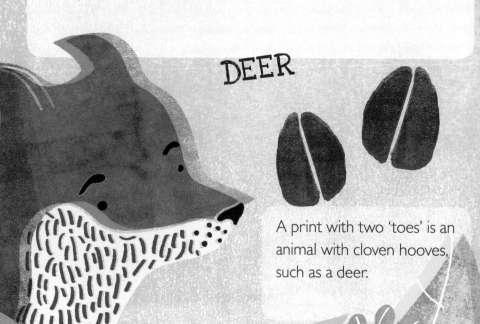

A print with two 'toes' is an animal with cloven hooves, such as a deer.

CAT

Cats can pull in their claws, so their paw prints won't have dots in front of the toes.

Be a plant expert

A botanist is a plant expert, and some botanists explore the world looking for new and exotic plants. New plants are given names based on their colour, characteristics, who found them, and so on. This naming system was invented way back in 1735 by a Swedish scientist called Carl Linnaeus. This same stystem is still used by botanists today.

You can be a botanist too! Find a flower in the woods and give it a name. For example, if it's yellow, and has four petals and smells like vanilla, call it 'Yellowvanilla fourpetalosa'.

'Yellowvanilla fourpetalosa'

Safety

Never eat unidentified berries – they may be poisonous. Always check with an adult.

Foraging for treats

Berries are a natural, tasty treat. They grow in brambles and hedgerows in the autumn. Watch out for scratchy thorns when you pick them, though. And remember, leave some behind for other people – and birds and wildlife – to enjoy!

Den Building

If you're playing in the woods, you've just got to build a den! There are loads of different ways to make a brilliant den, and this cool camouflaged hide-out is just one of them.

Construction tips

For the framework – you'll need to find two trees that are growing 3 or 4 metres apart, two large Y-shaped branches, and a long branch to be the cross-pole.

1 Prop the Y-shaped branches against the two trunks and then place the long cross-pole between the two Y-shaped branches.

2 Balance the branches at an angle against each side of the cross-pole to make the walls of your den. Don't forget to leave an entrance!

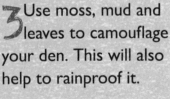

3 Use moss, mud and leaves to camouflage your den. This will also help to rainproof it.

4 A bed of dry leaves or cut hay makes a great carpet inside your den.

5 After all your hard work, you're ready to tuck into hot chocolate and marshmallows!

YOU WILL NEED

- For the sides – lots of largish branches, roughly the same size
- For weather-proofing – masses of moss and mud
- For camouflaging – armfuls of dry, crunchy leaves
- For nourishment – marshmallows and hot chocolate

Take a trunk...

Did you know you can work out the age of a cut-down tree by looking at its trunk? Just count the number of rings — there is one ring for each year of a tree's life. Can you work out how old this tree was before it was cut down? There are a lot of rings to count!

You could try a teepee-style den, too!

Go green

Be kind to nature and use building materials that are already on the ground, rather than breaking branches and twigs off plants and trees.

Eco Art

Great works of art don't have to be made on a piece of paper. Land art uses the natural materials around us – like moss, twigs, branches, leaves, stones and rocks – to make awesome art, and anyone can do it, anywhere!

I love hearts and spirals

Collect piles of woodland treasures such as small stones, fir cones, conkers or leaves. Clear a space and then use your treasure to create gorgeous geometric shapes.

Marvellous moss monster

Create an awesome moss monster using a mossy log for the body, and twigs and branches for the arms. What could you use for your monster's eyes?

Autumn leaf chain

Carefully thread pretty autumn leaves together to make a delicate leaf chain. To thread the leaves, make a small slit in the bottom half of a leaf and push the stalk of the second leaf through it. You can make the chain secure by then weaving the stalk back through the leaf, ending with the stalk at the back of the chain. Work from the largest leaf down to the smallest. Hang the chain from a tree to catch the sunlight — and leave for the next passer-by to enjoy!

Go green

Be a respectful land artist by making sure you don't damage any plants when you hunt for your art materials.

Land art fact

There are many talented land artists who use natural materials to create amazing art. One is Robert Smithson, who created the beautiful Spiral Jetty at the Great Salt Lake in Utah, USA. This incredible structure is made out of mud, rocks and salt crystals, and is over 450 metres long and 4.5 metres wide.

watch it Blow!

Stand with your eyes closed and feel the wind blowing around you. You might not be able to see the wind, but you can certainly feel it!

Leaf catcher

Play this game on a windy autumn day. Keep your eyes on the skies, and when the wind blows, try to catch any falling leaves before they hit the ground. If you are playing with other people, the winner is the person who catches the most!

Roaring dragon windsock

A windsock shows the direction the wind is blowing, and this dragon one does it with style!

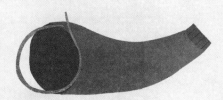

1 Cut a sleeve off at the shoulder seam. Bend the wire into a circle, the same size as the top of the sleeve.

2 Ask an adult to help you fold over 2cm of fabric to cover the wire, and then stitch the wire in place.

3 Your dragon has a mouth! Cut the felt to create eyes and a few scales, and sew on.

4 Take the leftover fabric, and cut out a square to make a 'pocket' for the stone.

The stone helps keep the windsock facing into the wind.

5 With the windsock inside out, attach the pocket where the dragon's 'chin' is, by sewing along three sides. Pop the stone inside, then sew the fourth side.

6 Turn the windsock back out the right way. Cut the string in half and sew the end of each piece to the sides of the dragon's mouth.

7 Tie your windsock to a high branch. Your dragon will show you the direction the wind is blowing from!

Musical Airs...

Have you ever listened to the amazing sounds the wind makes? It whistles, wails and howls…You can use the power of the wind to make other noises, too!

- Metal cutlery (with a ridge where the handle joins the blade)
- Long pipe cleaners (1 for each piece of cutlery)
- Beads
- String
- Scissors
- A small branch on a tree
- An adult helper

Cutlery wind chime

Wind chimes are outdoor mobiles. The dangling bits make jangling noises as the wind knocks them together. You can make this simple wind chime using old metal cutlery.

1 Knot the end of a pipe cleaner around the top of the handle of a piece of cutlery, leaving a long end of pipe cleaner sticking out.

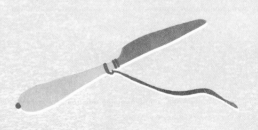

Jingle shells

Hunt out seashells and pebbles with holes in them. Thread string through the holes, tying a knot to secure each pebble and shell. In between them, thread some beads and knot in place. Repeat with more pieces of string. Tie the strings to a coat hanger, about 2.5cm apart, and hang them outside, then listen to the shells jingle in the wind!

2 Add a bead to the pipe cleaner, and then wind the pipe cleaner around the handle, adding beads as you go. End on a large bead, and knot the pipe cleaner around the cutlery to secure it.

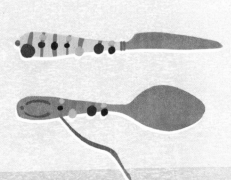

3 Repeat steps 1 and 2 with each piece of cutlery. Then knot a 30cm piece of string around the top bead on each piece.

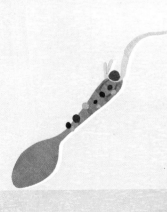

4 Tie each piece of cutlery to the branch. Hang them close enough that the wind will knock them together.

Windy Day Play

The wind is great for keeping things moving – kites, boats, leaves… and you! Get on the move with some wild windy day play.

Wobbly jellyfish kite

You make the jellyfish… and the wind will make it wobble!

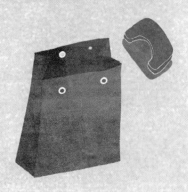

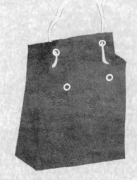

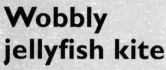
1 Flatten the bag and punch two holes at the top (open) end, about 2.5cm down and 2.5cm in from the corners. Stick hole reinforcers on both sides of the four holes.

2 Cut one of the pieces of string in half. Create a handle on each side of the bag by threading the string through the holes, from the outside in, and knotting securely.

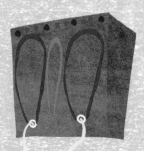

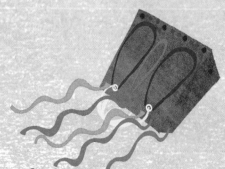

4 Decorate the bag body of your jellyfish using coloured pens.

5 Stick paper streamers to the lower section of the paper bag to make tentacles.

Leaf-sail boat race

Sailing boats need wind to power them, and so do cute little leaf-sail boats!

They are easy to make with a piece of bark for the boat, a strong twig for the mast and a large leaf for the sail. Carefully thread the twig through the leaf to make a sail, and push the twig mast through the bark. Find a stream or large puddle, and your boat is ready to race!

3 Loop one end of the second piece of string through both handles and tie in a knot.

Lean into a gust of wind, arms out, like a bird.

A really strong wind will support you very briefly!

6 Once the glue is dry... your kite is ready to fly!

Hello Rain!

When the rain starts, the outdoor fun doesn't have to stop. There's still tons of great stuff to do outside – you can measure the rain, splash in it, even lie down and make art in it!

Rain shadows

If it's starting to rain, don't rush inside… stay and make rain shadows! Pick a safe spot – such as your patio, or a path in the park, and lie down when the rain starts. Stay still while the rain wets the ground around you – when you get up, there will be a dry area which is your rain shadow.

You can make great rain shadows from other objects too, like your bike or scooter. The best shadows are made on stone or tarmac.

Be a weather expert

A meteorologist is an expert who collects information about the weather. You can be one too, by using your rain catcher (opposite) to measure how much rain is falling when there's a heavy shower. How about when it's just a light shower? Try comparing the amount of rain to the length of time the shower lasted.

Rain catcher

Ever wondered how much rain is really falling?
This rain catcher lets you measure exactly that!

YOU WILL NEED

- A clear plastic drinks bottle (without a lid)
- Scissors
- Stickers
- Permanent markers
- Clear waterproof varnish
- Brush
- Long wooden spoon
- Ruler
- 2 x thick pipe cleaners
- Gravel
- An adult helper

1 Ask an adult to help you cut the top off the bottle, about three-quarters of the way up. You will need the top for step 5.

2 Decorate the bottle using stickers and marker pens, then ask an adult to cover it with a layer of varnish.

3 Lay the spoon down next to the ruler. Starting 1cm up, mark cm lines along the handle using a marker pen.

4 Draw a face on the front of the spoon. Make a 'jumper' by winding a pipe cleaner around the neck of the spoon. Use another pipe cleaner to make arms.

5 Fill the bottom of the bottle with gravel, and slot the upside-down top of the bottle inside your decorated bottle.

6 Place your rain catcher in an open spot in your garden. After a rain shower, dip your rain man measure in to see how much rain has fallen!

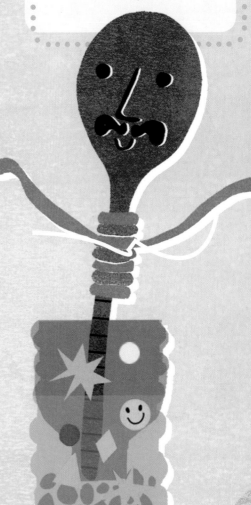

Rain Painting

A rainy day doesn't have to be a wash out – it can be a great opportunity to get arty, and you can even use the rain water in your art!

Beat it!

Hapa Zome is the Japanese art of beating leaves and flowers to pound their natural colours into cloth. The more moisture there is in the leaves and flowers the better the result will be – ones picked just after a rain shower are perfect!

1 Fold the cloth in half and make a crease line. Open up the cloth and use the leaves and flowers to make a design on just the right-hand side of the crease.

2 Fold the left side of the cloth over to cover the design. Ask an adult to help you gently pound the cloth with a mallet or stone.

3 Carefully open up the cloth to reveal your image. You can then frame it to create a special gift.

Raindrop art

Mud, food colouring and charcoal work just as well as paint when it comes to making rain pictures. Just make blobs on a large piece of paper and leave outside in the rain. Watch from a window to see how the rain transforms the blobs. Bring your picture in when you like the way it looks and lay it down flat to dry.

Tracing and racing

When you sit inside on a cold day have you ever noticed the layer of water droplets – called condensation – on the inside of the window? You can use your finger to trace a picture in this moisture. Then if you put a piece of coloured paper over the traced picture, the paper picks up the wet areas and the picture you traced with your finger stays dry. Magic!

Raindrop races

Have a raindrop race with a friend. Both choose a water droplet at the top of a window, and see which one reaches the bottom first!

Splish, Splosh!

Don't stay indoors listening to the sound of the rain… Get outside with friends and put together a raindrop orchestra. With pots and pans and sticks and spoons you'll soon be making more noise than the rain!

Set the stage

If you know there's a heavy downpour due, place different containers outside ready to catch the rain. Mix it up by using plastic and metal pots in a range of different sizes.

Sounds like…

Huge containers and tiny containers filled with water make different sounds. Try adding or reducing the amount of water in a pot to change the sound it makes.

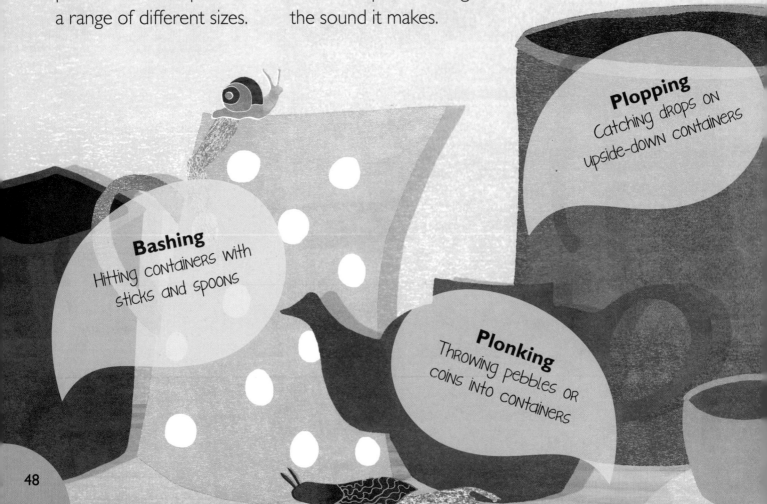

Plopping
Catching drops on upside-down containers

Bashing
Hitting containers with sticks and spoons

Plonking
Throwing pebbles or coins into containers

Go green

Don't waste the rainwater you have collected – put it to good use by storing it to water thirsty plants on a dry day. (Or you could use it to fill the water bombs on page 56!)

Splashing
Jumping in a puddle could be the sound to end your tune!

Sloshing
Stirring water around in containers

Whooshing
Tipping water between containers

Sun Time

People have used sundials to tell the time for thousands of years. Building your own super cool sundial is a fun project for the whole family to work on together in the sunshine.

Super sundial

A sundial uses the position of the sun in the sky to show the time. It has a face and a dial hand that casts a shadow showing how the position of the sun changes from hour to hour.

Plant pots mark the hours 1 to 12.

YOU WILL NEED

- Chalk
- Tape measure
- 1m bamboo cane
- 1 x 20cm terracotta pot (empty)
- Gravel
- Chalks/paints
- 4 x 25cm terracotta pots (filled with plants)
- 8 x 10cm terracotta pots (empty)
- An adult helper

1 Choose your spot – a sunny patio is perfect. Ask an adult to help you chalk out a 1.2m square base. Then carefully chalk a circle inside the base that touches all the sides of the square.

2 To make the dial, stick the bamboo cane in the 20cm pot and pack gravel around it to hold it upright. Then place the pot in the centre of the square base.

3 Using chalk or paint, mark the four large plant pots with the quarter hours of a clock (12, 3, 6, 9).

4 Turn the eight smallest pots upside down and mark them with the remaining hours (1, 2, 4, 5, 7, 8, 10, 11).

5 Each hour, on the hour, check the position of the shadow cast by the cane, and make sure that the the pot for that time is in the correct place (under the shadow).

The shadow from the bamboo cane shows the time!

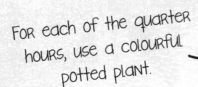

For each of the quarter hours, use a colourful potted plant.

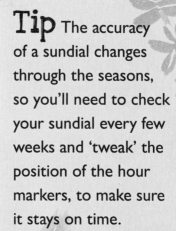

Tip The accuracy of a sundial changes through the seasons, so you'll need to check your sundial every few weeks and 'tweak' the position of the hour markers, to make sure it stays on time.

Cloud Spotting

Got your head in the clouds? That's not so bad – they are pretty amazing! Clouds are made of tiny droplets of water, and they come in all sorts of shapes and sizes.

3-D cloud portraits

Beautiful clouds have inspired artists throughout history. But painting a flat picture of clouds is boring – painting a 3-D picture is much more impressive! Mix one cup of shaving foam with one cup of white glue in a bowl to make thick, fluffy 'paint'. Blob this onto paper and shape with a spoon to make 3-D clouds that stay puffy when dry.

YOU WILL NEED

- Shaving foam
- White glue
- Coloured paper
- A spoon

Tip Add coloured paint or food colouring to your shaving foam and glue mixture to make pink and yellow sunset clouds. Pretty!

Be a cloud expert

A nepholographer studies and photographs clouds. If you have a camera, you can be one too! Find a cloud you like the look of, take a photograph and print it out. What shape can you see in your cloud? An animal, a person or a pattern? Sketch in the outline of the shape and then stick it on your wall or send it as a card to a friend!

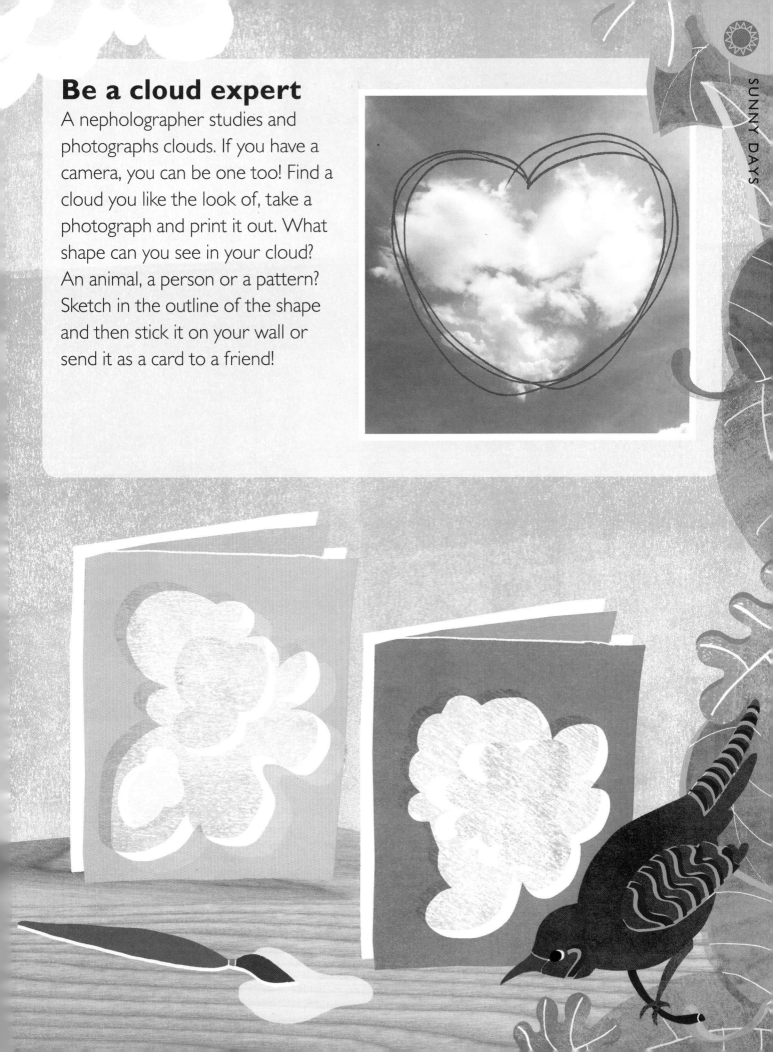

Sun Printing

You'll be surprised by just how powerful the sun's rays can be. They can even print a picture in a couple of hours – with your help of course!

Sunshine reverse stencil

Use the sun to help you create an original and totally hot t-shirt design!

1 Cut the card sheets so they are just bigger than your t-shirt. Carefully draw around the outline of your t-shirt on one sheet of card.

2 Tape your t-shirt to the other sheet of card. Make sure the t-shirt is in the same position as for step 1.

3 Take the first sheet of card and draw a sun design onto the centre of the t-shirt outline.

4 Ask an adult to carefully cut the design out of the sheet of card using the craft knife.

5 Sandwich the two sheets of card together and fasten the edges with clothes pegs. Lay them in the sun for several days.

Sunshine silhouettes

On a sunny day get busy with some dark-coloured construction paper and an interesting selection of small, solid objects. Maybe coins, pebbles, leaves… or anything else you like the shape of!

Arrange the objects into a design on the paper, then place in full sunlight – outdoors or on a windowsill – and leave for at least an hour. When the paper has faded, remove the objects to reveal a fab sunshine silhouette. The longer you leave your design sunbathing, the better the result will be!

6 Open up the card… and see the sunshine on your t-shirt!

Safety The sun's rays are mega powerful! Always remember to protect your skin while you're outdoors by wearing sun protection, and never look directly at the sun.

Water Fight!

You don't need water pistols for a top water fight! There's an arsenal of water blasters ready and waiting around your home, and you can even make your own water bombs!

For the best water fights...

＊ It can get slippy, so find a large, safe area to play in.

＊ Always ask permission before you turn your garden into a splash arena!

Bombs away!

Making your own water bombs is fun – and throwing them is even better!

WATER FIGHT KIT LIST

Buckets
Essential for holding your water supplies

Sponges
Perfect super-soakers for drenching in one good splat!

Squeezy bottles
For a direct squirt that hits the spot!

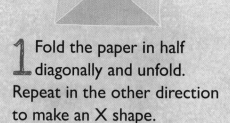

1 Fold the paper in half diagonally and unfold. Repeat in the other direction to make an X shape.

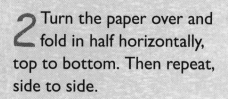

2 Turn the paper over and fold in half horizontally, top to bottom. Then repeat, side to side.

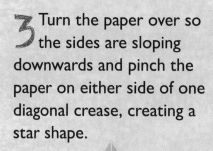

3 Turn the paper over so the sides are sloping downwards and pinch the paper on either side of one diagonal crease, creating a star shape.

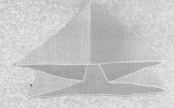

4 Carefully flatten down into one triangle shape.

5 Take the bottom corners on the front side and fold them up to the top in the middle. Repeat on the back to make a square.

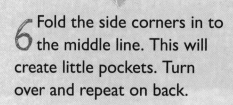

6 Fold the side corners in to the middle line. This will create little pockets. Turn over and repeat on back.

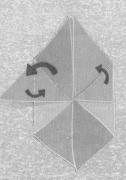

7 Fold the flap above each pocket out to the side, then fold it back in half to the centre, to make a smaller, triangular flap.

8 This flap should then fit neatly inside the pocket. Repeat on the other sides.

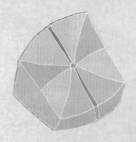

9 Blow in the hole in the bottom to inflate, then fill with water.

Tasty Treats

Sunny days are made for eating outdoors – and cooking outdoors, too. So let's set up the campfire kitchen and get those taste buds zinging!

YOU WILL NEED

- 8 oranges
- Sharp knife
- Large spoon
- 1 mix for chocolate brownie cake (plus the extra ingredients on the packet)
- Mixing bowl
- Wooden spoon
- Foil
- 8 teaspoons
- Campfire
- An adult helper

Orange-pot campfire choccy cake

Nothing beats food cooked on a campfire! Next time you're having a campfire cookout try this delicious dessert – gooey chocolate brownie cakes baked inside oranges.

1 Ask an adult to slice the tops off the oranges and then scoop out the flesh with a large spoon.

2 Prepare the brownie cake mix according to the packet instructions.

Safety

Campfire cooking is fun but can be dangerous! Make sure an adult is supervising at all times.

Sun-dried apple rings

You'll need some peeled, cored apples, sliced into rings about half a centimetre thick – ask an adult to help you with this. Lay the rings on a tray with holes in it, and place the tray in a sunny spot raised up on a couple of bricks, so that air can circulate. Cover the fruit with a teatowel to protect it from bugs and birds. Leave it to dry it for several days, turning the rings twice a day and bringing them in at night. Check the fruit is ready by tearing a ring in half – it should feel rubbery. Then tuck in and enjoy!

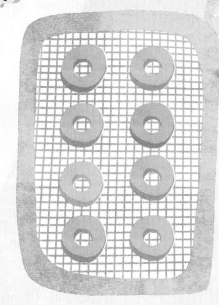

3 Fill each orange 'pot' with brownie batter, leaving 2.5cm at the top.

4 Add the orange 'lids' and tightly wrap each orange in at least two layers of foil.

5 Ask an adult to put them in the campfire embers for around 40 minutes, turning them every so often.

6 Carefully unwrap… and dig in!

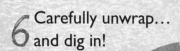

Tip Use the flesh from the oranges to flavour the brownie mix!

I Spy...

The beach is a brilliant place to see weird and wonderful wildlife. And while paddling in a rock pool when the tide's out, who knows what you may find!

Bird clues

You may see birds at the beach that are different from the ones you see in your garden. Some detective work can help you identify them. Draw or photograph each bird and note down their size and the colour of their feathers, feet and beak. Hunt around for physical clues like feathers and tracks in the sand. Back at home, research your bird online or in a bird-spotting book.

Natural nibbles

What are the birds at the beach eating? Worms, like the birds in your garden, or maybe something different?

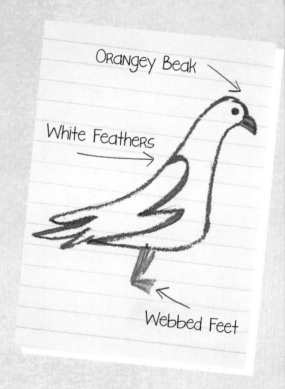

Orangey Beak

White Feathers

Webbed Feet

Bird fact

Many birds that live near water have webbed feet to help them swim. These act like flippers, pushing through the water as they swim.

Rock pool world

There's a world of living creatures to discover in even the smallest rock pool. Grab a net and a bucket and dip in!

To be a top rock pool explorer:

* When dipping your hands in be careful you don't get nibbled!

* Put creatures straight into water while you take a closer look at them.

* Handle creatures with care and return them to where you found them.

* Always use a net to 'fish out' creatures.

* Don't pull at bits of seaweed – it can take years for it to grow back!

Safety

Stay safe – make sure an adult is keeping an eye out for the tide coming back in.

Dam Building

Have you ever paddled in a stream and felt the pressure of the water as it whooshes past your feet? Well, get ready to stop that water in its tracks!

Get building!

Dams are used to make sure the right amount of water is at the right place at the right time. The dam blocks the flow of the river, so the water builds up behind it to form a large lake, called a reservoir. The reservoir water is used by houses, factories and farms.

You can find loads of things to build your dam near the stream itself – twigs, branches, rocks, stones, gravel and mud. The more friends you have to muck in with the dam building, the better.

Always remember to remove the dam before you leave and return everything as you found it.

YOU WILL NEED

- Large stones
- Smaller stones and gravel
- Mud
- Small branches and twigs

Large stones are essential for a sturdy base.

Criss-crossed twigs, mud and gravel fill any small holes.

Be an engineer

An engineer is someone who designs and builds things – machines, roads, bridges, dams and more – and you can be one too! While you're building your dam, think about its design and the materials you are using. Which materials hold back the water best? What happens if you change the design? Try using the smaller stones on the bottom and the larger ones on top and see what happens.

Step by step

Hunt for some sturdy stones to make your own stepping stone path across the stream. Secure the stones by digging a base for them in the stream bed, and then pack them in with gravel and pebbles. Make sure they're not wobbly, then get stepping!

Add strips of bark for the finishing touch.

Safety

Never play in water unattended. Ask an adult to help you find a shallow stream that's safe to play in.

Pebble Play

There are tons of cool games you can play on a pebbly beach – you can even practise becoming a super skimmer!

Skimming stones

Find a safe place to stand at the edge of a calm sea or lake and have your stones at the ready. See who can make their stones 'bounce' the most times across the water. Award a shell or pebble for every bounce a player gets. The player with the most bounces wins!

Skim like a pro

Smooth, flat stones the size of the palm of your hand make the best skimmers.

Balance the stone on top of your middle finger and use your thumb and forefinger to spin the stone through the air.

Get as low down to the ground as you can and throw straight out, keeping your stone as close to the water as possible.

Before you throw, always check there are no swimmers or birds nearby!

Pebble pics

Get busy collecting pebbles that are the same colour – dark grey ones, snowy white ones, coral-coloured ones. Then use them to create your own seaside creature on the beach!

Bottle bashing

Bury an empty plastic bottle 5cm deep in the sand. Players take it in turns to throw pebbles at the bottle until either it falls over – or if you are timing each turn, the time runs out!

Go green

Make sure you take the plastic bottle home with you and recycle it.

Seaside Souvenirs

If you know where to look, the seashore is a trove brimming with treasure! Grab a bucket and get hunting for little gems such as pretty shells, wave-softened glass, shiny seaweed and colourful starfish.

I see seashells

Big ones, tiny ones, swirly ones – the beach is awash with amazing shells! But did you know that these shells are the homes of small creatures called molluscs? If you find a living creature in one of the shells you collect, be sure to return it to a safe spot like a rock pool.

Be a rock expert

A geologist is an expert who studies rocks and minerals, which is what sand is made from. To be a geologist yourself, take a close look at some sand. You might see tiny bits of brown or white quartz or pink coral. Back at home, pour vinegar on your sand. If any of the grains give off tiny bubbles, they were once alive and are actually tiny pieces of coral, bone or shell!

Driftwood decoration

Having this funky decoration hanging around will remind you of the fun you had on the beach!

1 Ask an adult to help you skewer a hole in the top of the driftwood. Make a short string loop and knot securely.

2 Draw a simple, striking design on the driftwood. Something seaside-themed would be perfect!

3 Following the marker lines, carefully glue the shells and pebbles in place.

4 Hang up your decoration and enjoy your seaside memories!

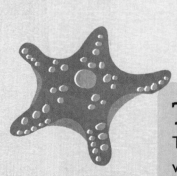

Tip

To clean empty shells, soak them in warm water and gently brush with an old, soft toothbrush.

Our Green Street

A team of neighbours working together can transform a street into a lush oasis, bursting with plants and flowers. Here are some ways you could green up your own neighbourhood…

Window boxes

Check if the window box will be in the sun or shade, and choose colourful plants that are suitable for those conditions. Adding hanging plants – such as tumbling tomatoes and sugar snap peas – will make your window box look, smell and taste fantastic!

GET PERMISSION

Before you create anything in a public space, even something green and beautiful, you need to have permission from your neighbours, and whoever owns the land. Ask an adult to help you arrange this.

Be a guerrilla gardener

Guerrilla gardeners plant flowers and vegetables on uncared-for spots in towns and cities. You can be a guerrilla gardener by making seedbombs. Throw your seedbombs onto grassy spots that need cheering up. The seeds will grow into flowers that look great – and will also attract wildlife to your neighbourhood!

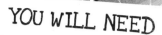

Seedbombing

Seedbombs are easy to make…
and fantastic to launch!

YOU WILL NEED

- 3 tablespoons of clay powder
- 6 tablespoons of compost
- Bowl
- 1 teaspoon of wildflower seeds
- Water
- Tray
- Tissue paper

1 Use your hands to mix the clay powder and compost in a bowl then add a teaspoon of seeds and mix again.

2 Add small amounts of water to form a paste. Split the paste into six bits.

3 Between flat palms, roll six balls and place them on a tray covered in tissue paper.

4 Dry the seedbombs in a warm, dark place (like an airing cupboard) for 24 hours.

5 Check the weather and if rain is forecast, it's the perfect time to go seedbombing!

Tip Store your dried seedbombs in an airtight container in a dark place until you are ready to launch them.

Street Art

Your street is a blank canvas, waiting to be livened up by eco-friendly art. Transform it using coloured chalks, moss, and a lot of imagination but ask permission first!

Chalk art

Pavement art is easy to create using coloured chalks, and washes off when you are done, but don't forget to ask permission before you get creative! Wow your neighbours with your artistic creations, or have fun drawing around your friends' outlines.

Just an illusion...

With a bunch of chalks and a heap of skill, street artists can create amazing 3-D pavement art that looks real enough to fall into or climb up! These talented artists have an amazing ability to trick the eyes of passers-by into seeing 3-D images on a completely flat surface. It takes time to create… but the impact is incredible!

Grow your own graffiti

In many urban spaces you'll see colourful graffiti sprayed or stencilled on walls, buildings and bridges. Moss graffiti is an eco-friendly way of growing art on an outdoor wall. Make sure it's one you have permission to paint!

YOU WILL NEED

- 350ml water
- 60ml yoghurt or buttermilk
- ½ teaspoon sugar
- A big handful of moss
- Blender
- Small bucket
- Chalk
- Paintbrush
- An unpainted, textured outdoor wall you have permission to paint
- Water spray
- An adult helper

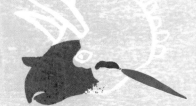

1 Add the water, yoghurt or buttermilk, sugar and moss to the blender. Blend until smooth.

2 Add the mixture to a bucket. Chalk a design onto the wall and then colour it in using the mixture.

3 Spray with water daily for several weeks and then once weekly to keep your graffiti alive.

Watch your graffiti grow!

Tip If you want to change the design, you can remove your moss graffiti by spraying it with lime juice.

Urban Safari

You don't have to be trekking through the Amazon to see wild and wonderful things. Whether you live in a concrete jungle or leafy suburbia, take a walk on the wild side down the streets of your neighbourhood!

Wildlife zone

Choose an area to explore – maybe a few streets around your home. Take a camera, pen and paper so you can keep a record of what, where and when you make a find in your wildlife zone. Pay close attention to what's on the ground. If you turn over stones and bits of wood you may find prehistoric woodlice and other creepy crawlies. Be careful when you put the stone back not to crush any insects.

Urban Safari this way ⟩⟩⟩⟩

Safari spot

Make a list of types of urban wildlife to spot, and come up with a scoring system. Easy-to-find things have lower points and trickier-to-find things have higher points. Each player has their own list and a pencil. Tick animals off when you spot them. You can play during the day or at night — just adjust your list to suit the time of day. Here are some ideas to get you started…

Safari Hit List

Bug life	POINTS
Single insect	5
Insect nest or web	10
Pollinator in action	15

Tweet, tweet	
Seeing a bird	5
Hearing a bird	10
Seeing a bird feeding	15

What am I?	
Small mammal	2
Large mammal	5
Amphibian	10
Reptile	20
Out of the Zone!	50

FOR a spot that's out of its natural habitat, like a cliff-nesting seabird on a city rooftop!

Street Party

Even parties are better outdoors! A street party is a great way to bring your neighbourhood together, with yummy things to eat and drink and plenty of fun activities. Let's get the party started!

Getting organised

You'll need to ask the grown-ups to talk to the council where you live to arrange to close off the street. Once that's been done and the date is set, you can get busy making sure the party goes with a swing…

Decide on a theme
It could be a general theme, like animals, or a theme based around the name of your street, or something your neighbourhood is known for.

Make and deliver invites
Include important information like the theme, date and time, and what people should bring.

Make bunting and flags
Create a festival atmosphere by recycling old clothes or curtains to make colourful bunting and flags.

Tables and chairs
Speak to your neighbours and see who can bring what – garden furniture is ideal for a street party, and gazebos are useful, too.

Food and drink
Draw up a list of yummy food and drink you'll need and ask each family to bring something from it.

Make music
Get together a box of musical instruments – maracas and whistles always help get a party started!

Activity ideas...

There are tons of great activities you can do at your street party to bring everyone together. Here are just a few suggestions to get you thinking...

Get sporty!

Get your street party off to an energetic start:

* egg-and-spoon races

* sack races

* three-legged races

* tug of war

You could also learn some circus skills – see if any of your neighbours can juggle, and ask them to teach you!

Get arty!

The creative fun doesn't have to stop at making bunting:

* colourful chalk murals

* funky face masks

* face painting

* portrait painting

Get thinking...

Draw up some questions for a quiz. You could base them around some of these ideas:

* the street's history

* the street's families

* the party theme

* general knowledge

You could have each family as a team, and don't forget to arrange a prize for the winner!

Why not see how many of the activities and adventures in this book you can incorporate into your street party? Introduce your neighbourhood to the Outdoor Wonderland!

Discover More

Take a look through this selection of websites for more top tips, fascinating facts and incredible inspiration for having outdoor fun!

IN THE GARDEN

Find out more

Bee facts and identification tips
www.pestworldforkids.org/bees.html

Getting wildlife in your garden
http://www.wildaboutgardens.org.uk/things-to-do.aspx

What else can I do?

Make a cool bird scarer
http://readyforten.com/users/RFTdeb/posts/5188-how-to-make-a-bird-scarer)

Plant a vegetable garden
www.homeandgardensite.com/ChildrensSite/vegetable_garden.htm/

IN THE NIGHT-TIME

Find out more

Sunrise and sunset times worldwide
www.timeanddate.com/worldclock/sunrise.html

The moon's phases – using Oreo biscuits!
spaceplace.nasa.gov/oreo-moon/en/

When to see meteor showers
stardate.org/nightsky/meteors

What else can I do?

Identify animals at night
www.kidsplanet.org/games/js/whoami.html

Join international dawn chorus day
www.idcd.info

Play astronomy games and activities
www.kidsastronomy.com/index.htm /

IN THE PARK

Find out more

Photographing wildlife
www.bbc.co.uk/nature/22115362
121clicks.com/tag/famous-wildlife-photographers

What else can I do?

Super snail racing
www.thingamababy.com/baby/2007/11/snailrace.html

Raise your own butterfly
www.kidsbutterfly.org/faq/catching/4/

IN THE WOODS

Find out more

Terrific tree facts and figures
http://www.savatree.com/tree-facts.html

What else can I do?

Build a fab den
www.edenproject.com/blog/index.php/2011/06/how-to-build-your-own-den/

Make some land art
www.letthechildrenplay.net/2010/08/land-art-for-kids.html

WINDY DAYS

Find out more

Why the wind blows and other facts!
www.weatherwizkids.com/weather-wind.htm

What else can I do?

Make a simple weather vane
www.sciencekids.co.nz/projects/windvane.html

RAINY DAYS

Find out more

Why it rains and other cool facts!
www.weatherwizkids.com/weather-rain

Measuring rain
www.skyriderforkids.com/doubletakes/yellow/dt_
yellow_rainfall.html

What else can I do?

Make a mud pie
www.ntsouthwest.co.uk/2013/07/13-make-a-mud-pie/

SUNNY DAYS

Find out more

How a sundial tells the time
www.liverpoolmuseums.org.uk/kids/games-quizzes/sun/
san5.html

What clouds are made of
www.weatherwizkids.com/weather-clouds.htm

What else can I do?

Make a daisy chain
www.wikihow.com/Make-a-Daisy-Chain

Cook some campfire food
www.kids-cooking-activities.com/kids-campfire-cooking.
html

BY THE WATER

Find out more

Fascinating facts on dams and beavers
www.sciencekids.co.nz/sciencefacts/engineering/dams.
html

kids.nationalgeographic.co.uk/kids/animals/
creaturefeature/beavers/

Rocking rock pools – what to look for
www.bbc.co.uk/nature/habitats/Tide_pool

What else can I do?

Play Pooh sticks
www.pooh-sticks.com/content/rules

Make a pond viewer!
www.hometrainingtools.com/pond-life/a/1516/

IN THE STREET

Find out more

Seedbombs and guerilla gardening
www.seedfreedom.net/

Street art facts and amazing 3D art!
news.bbc.co.uk/cbbcnews/hi/uk/
newsid_1973000/1973430.stm

www.mediagang.co.uk/3d-street-art-examples

What else can I do?

Make some online street art
kids.tate.org.uk/games/street-art/

Build a city birdbath
fun.familyeducation.com/activity/birds/39472.html

Index

CREDITS

The publishers would like to thank the
following for permission to reproduce
the following photographs in the book:

p16 Shutterstock/Hintau Aliaksei

p23 [T] NASA; [B] Shutterstock/Shalygin

p24–25 Fotolia

p31 [T] Shutterstock/Yellowj; [M] Shutterstock/leungchopan; [B]
Shutterstock/Michael G. Mill

p33 Shutterstock/ Alex Staroseltsev;
Shutterstock/as3

p35 Shutterstock/ Ivan Smuk

p37 Shutterstock/Eric Broder Van Dyke

p38 Fotolia

p44 Shutterstock/Andrew Chin

p47 Shutterstock/ natuska

p53 Fotolia/Christas Vengel

p63 Shutterstock/Anatoly Kovtun

p70 Shutterstock/hans engbers